"*Women, Work, and Calling* should be on the bookshelf of any female leader seeking to utilize her gifts and ambitions in ways that serve colleagues and honor God. The inspirational stories and practical advice will help women fulfill the unique work God calls them to with a sense of joy and confidence."

Cammie Dunaway, former chief marketing officer of Duolingo, Nintendo, and Yahoo!

"In *Women, Work, and Calling*, Joanna Meyer draws on years of listening to women who work, paying attention to the complexity of their calling as they wrestle with the question, What is my work and what does it mean? Biblically born, experientially rich, attentive to the most contemporary questions about what life and labor require of us, this grounded, thoughtful meditation gives us a window into what it means to be a woman at work in the world, a perennial challenge for daughters of Eve at any time and in any place."

Steven Garber, senior fellow for vocation and the common good at the M. J. Murdock Charitable Trust and author of *The Seamless Life: A Tapestry of Love and Learning, Worship and Work*

"For Christian women who have been made to feel as though your place in the story of God is small—this book is for you. Joanna Meyer is here to declare that God welcomes you into a bigger, brighter, more hope-filled story about how much your work matters."

Michaela O'Donnell, author of *Make Work Matter* and the Mary and Dale Andringa Executive Director Chair at the Max De Pree Center for Leadership

"In our ever-changing culture, women need wisdom and support as they press ahead in the professional realm as disciples of Jesus. Joanna Meyer offers just that with depth and care. *Women, Work, and Calling* is a resource I wish I'd had earlier in my career."

Melissa K. Russell, North America regional president of International Justice Mission

"In this much-needed book, Joanna Meyer explores internal and external challenges that Christian women face in the workplace. In short and accessible chapters appropriate for individuals or groups, Meyer draws on Scripture, social science research, and the voices of Christian leaders to provide guidance for navigating these challenges. I highly recommend this book for women at every career stage, from the college student to the seasoned professional, and everyone in between."

Denise Daniels, Hudson T. Harrison Professor of Entrepreneurship at Wheaton College

"A perfect handbook for the woman of faith struggling to discover, claim, and ignite her calling. With a bold invitation to get to it—but also why and how—accomplished leader Joanna Meyer sets down a clear theological road map for making a woman's calling not just a dream but a God-blessed reality. Now, soar!"

Patricia Raybon, author of the Annalee Spain Mystery series and *I Told the Mountain to Move*

"I've long admired Joanna Meyer for her insights on vocation. She's done the hard work and deep thinking to become an expert on the intersection of women, work, and calling. Joanna generously shares that knowledge with us in *Women, Work, and Calling*. This accessible and immediately applicable storehouse of wisdom is unapologetically biblical, challenging the heart and mind."

Eric Schumacher, coauthor of *Worthy* and *Jesus and Gender* with Elyse Fitzpatrick

"Thank God for Joanna Meyer! Her book is essential reading for Christian women and those who want to see us make faithful and significant contributions as leaders in society. Every page of *Women, Work, and Calling* is a powerful contribution, full of biblically grounded thought, grace-filled writing, and practical wisdom."

Stephanie Summers, CEO of the Center for Public Justice

Women, Work & Calling

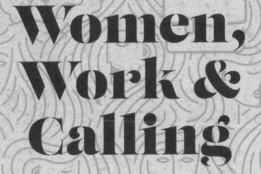

STEP INTO YOUR PLACE IN GOD'S WORLD

JOANNA MEYER

An imprint of InterVarsity Press
Downers Grove, Illinois

InterVarsity Press
P.O. Box 1400 | Downers Grove, IL 60515-1426
ivpress.com | email@ivpress.com

©2023 by Denver Institute for Faith & Work

InterVarsity Press® is the publishing division of InterVarsity Christian Fellowship/USA®. For more information, visit intervarsity.org.

All Scripture quotations, unless otherwise indicated, are taken from The Holy Bible, New International Version®, NIV®. Copyright © 1973, 1978, 1984, 2011 by Biblica, Inc.™ Used by permission of Zondervan. All rights reserved worldwide. www.zondervan.com. The "NIV" and "New International Version" are trademarks registered in the United States Patent and Trademark Office by Biblica, Inc.™

While any stories in this book are true, some names and identifying information may have been changed to protect the privacy of individuals.

The publisher cannot verify the accuracy or functionality of website URLs used in this book beyond the date of publication.

Cover design: David Fassett
Interior design: Jeanna Wiggins
Cover images: Getty Images: © Alpha-C, © Svetlana Shamshurina, © Nikita Landin, © DStarky,
    © CSA Images, © Katsumi Murouchi, © Jonathan Knowles, © daboost

ISBN 978-1-5140-0793-8 (print) | ISBN 978-1-5140-0794-5 (digital)

Printed in the United States of America ∞

Library of Congress Cataloging-in-Publication Data
Names: Meyer, Joanna, 1974- author.
Title: Women, work, and calling : step into your place in God's world /
   Joanna Meyer.
Description: Downers Grove, IL : IVP Books, [2023] | Includes
   bibliographical references.
Identifiers: LCCN 2023014516 (print) | LCCN 2023014517 (ebook) | ISBN
   9781514007938 (print) | ISBN 9781514007945 (digital)
Subjects: LCSH: Church work with women. | Christian women–Religious life.
   | Women employees–Religious life.
Classification: LCC BV4445 .M49 2023 (print) | LCC BV4445 (ebook) | DDC
   259.082–dc23/eng/20230531
LC record available at https://lccn.loc.gov/2023014516
LC ebook record available at https://lccn.loc.gov/2023014517

30 29 28 27 26 25 24 23 | 12 11 10 9 8 7 6 5 4 3 2 1

To the women of my family,

whose work as farmers, missionaries, educators,

nurses, and poets inspires my own.

And to Rachel and Brooke,

for whom the adventure of responding

to God's call has just begun.

Contents

Introduction

What women bring to the table is not simply a feminine touch,
but half of humanity's gifts, passions, and experiences.

KATELYN BEATY

"To be honest, I don't know any women like me . . ." It's a lament I hear often when asking career-minded Christian women to introduce me to faithful women in their network. This feeling of isolation isn't limited to career women—ask any stay-at-home mom how lonely her days can be, and you'll hear stories of carpooling and answering endless toddler questions—but Christian women pursuing professional careers feel it profoundly. And often, the place they feel most lonely is in their faith communities.[1] Maybe you can relate.

This loneliness flows from a critical gap in discipleship for Christian women. As our roles in public life have grown, the church's vision for women's work and calling has not grown with us. Women find themselves navigating expectations for their roles as wives and mothers, complex gender dynamics in the workplace, and social pressure to portray picture-perfect lives (thank you, Instagram). If the church will not disciple Christian women for influence in public life, the world is eager to fill that gap.

This is why I'm so passionate about the themes explored in this book. Since 2015, I've had the privilege of leading Denver Institute for Faith & Work's programming for Christian women about work and calling. My commitment flows from the belief that work plays a critical role in God's mission. As the *imago Dei,* we are made to reflect the image of a Creator God, and we join him in making something of the world. To demonstrate the breadth and nuance of God's character, we need women *and* men to be vitally engaged in workplaces, homes, and organizations across our communities, utilizing the full extent of their God-given gifts.

Let me say that more clearly. *The world needs who God made you to be.*

Our goal through this short book is to establish, inspire, and equip women to fully live your calling in response to God's love and in service to others. The various chapters offer a theological foundation, insight from some of our favorite female leaders, and practical principles you can apply to your work.

In part one, we establish a biblical framework for thinking about your various roles. We cut through the cultural baggage surrounding women's roles to help you understand your calling and what it means for your daily work.

Part two turns inward to help you build the spiritual and emotional strength you need to thrive in your roles. You will learn to balance confidence with godly humility as you tackle the limiting beliefs that hold you back. You will also discover ways God can use the circumstances of your work to shape your soul and character.

In part three, we get practical by addressing common challenges women face in their work and leadership. You'll learn to lead more authentically while addressing gender dynamics that affect women in professional settings. And in one of my favorite chapters, we'll introduce the theme of "vocational power," the unique mix of skills, relationships, and resources you already possess that will allow you to have a godly influence in your setting.

The book concludes in part four with a look at the relationships you need to grow a thriving network. We challenge you to become a relationally generous leader, the kind of woman who brings a life-giving presence to her sphere of influence.

I pray that God challenges, strengthens, and inspires you through each chapter and page! May you embrace all that God has made you to be.

PART ONE

Ignite Your Vocational Imagination

1

Called Together

*Then God said, "Let us make mankind in our image,
in our likeness, so that they may rule over the fish in the
sea and the birds in the sky, over the livestock and
all the wild animals, and over all the creatures
that move along the ground."*

*So God created mankind in his own image,
in the image of God he created them;
male and female he created them.*

*God blessed them and said to them, "Be fruitful
and increase in number; fill the earth and subdue it.
Rule over the fish in the sea and the birds in the sky and
over every living creature that moves on the ground."*

GENESIS 1:26-28

One of the highlights of Denver Institute's programming
is our annual business leaders' event, Business for the

Common Good. Entrepreneurs and executives from across the country gather to learn how God works through his people to build healthier companies, design products that solve the world's toughest challenges, and serve their communities through their work. The first few years that we hosted the event, we noticed that there were hardly any women who attended. As one male guest observed, "Yikes! This feels like an old boys' club. Surely there are women who would benefit from being part of this gathering." But the imbalance extended beyond this single event. Whether we were inviting people to join our board of directors, finding panelists for events, or asking leaders to mentor young professionals, it was a challenge to find women to participate.

Observing the gender disparity in our programming forced us to examine deeply rooted expectations about gender roles, leadership models, and workplace dynamics—a learning process that led to the development of this book. As our understanding of the challenges Christian women face as we live out our callings has grown, our commitment to inspire and equip you for your work became stronger every day.

This commitment flows from the belief that women are vital players in God's redemptive purposes. The earliest pages of Scripture place women at the heart of his plan. Genesis 1:26-28 emphasizes three themes with relevance for any Christian's work:

1. God, as the Creator, is a *worker*, and his work is *good*.

2. Men and women are created in God's image, *an image they bear together*.

3. God entrusts creation to men and women, that they would rule it wisely, help it become more fruitful, and multiply—not only through physical reproduction but also by developing material goods, social structures, and culture.

Theologically speaking, this call is referred to as the creation mandate and represents God's first instructions to humankind.

We reflect the glory of our Creator by being like him—creators who work, as men and women, together. "[It's] worth noting that this is God's intention from creation," says Denise Daniels, a professor of entrepreneurship at Wheaton College and scholar on faith, work, and gender.[1] When women hold back—when we neglect our God-given gifts and responsibilities—a critical piece of God's design is missing. Aspects of God's character will be hidden from the world, and the partnership between men and women is weakened.

This interdependence is what Paul is getting at: "Neither is the man without the woman, neither the woman without the man, in the Lord" (1 Corinthians 11:11 KJV), or as it's expressed in the New International Version, "In the Lord woman is not independent of man, nor is man independent of woman."

Authors Myk Habets and Beulah Wood elaborate: "The Pauline 'not without' suggests that the identity of one gender cannot be 'without' the other. Men cannot be defined simply as what 'women are not'; women cannot be defined simply as 'what men are not.'"[2] As the Bible sees it, no kind of human community— a family, a church, or a workplace—can thrive without men and women working together.

Denise Daniels points to research showing that organizations with both men and women in executive and board roles perform better financially and have fewer ethical violations than organizations dominated by a single gender.[3] Imagine how a similar impact could extend far beyond the workplace if women fully embodied their gifts in response to God's broad call to care for and develop the world. In the chapters that follow, we invite you to discover—or reaffirm—God's design, as you serve, lead, and influence others through your daily work.

REFLECT

What does being made and called to work together tell us about God's character and his design for human flourishing?

Think about your own work context. What do the men and women you work with have in common? What does each gender offer that is unique? What would be lost if either was missing?

2

A Gospel as Big as the World

For God was pleased to have all his fullness dwell in him,
and through him to reconcile to himself all things,
whether things on earth or things in heaven,
by making peace through his blood, shed on the cross.

COLOSSIANS 1:19-20

When Colossians 1 says that God is reconciling all things to himself through Christ's death and resurrection, we must take that seriously—all things means *ALL things.* Every corner of creation—from the classroom dynamics in your local elementary school, to the potholes on the roads you drive, to the art that hangs on the walls of a museum downtown—matters to God and is a place for his power to work. Jesus died to save individual lives, but he also died to restore any area of creation that has been marred by the effects of sin or isn't the way God intends it to be. God cares about each teacher, lawyer, doctor, or parent; he also cares about the fields of education, law, medicine, and the family. Simply put, the scope of the gospel is as broad as the needs of the world.

When viewed this way, our vision for the ways God works in the world expands and becomes even more compelling. Any woman or man whose life has been touched by the gospel has a role to play in God's redemptive plan. What a thought! Through our daily work, in whatever form it takes, we have been entrusted with a corner of creation that awaits God's loving influence. When viewed this way, our work becomes more than just a way to support ourselves financially. It becomes a response to God's love and sacrifice, offered in service to others. From this foundation, we celebrate the diverse strengths God gave women and encourage them to develop their influence in the world.

I love this broad vision of the gospel because it affirms every woman's work, rather than dividing us into camps of women who work in professional contexts or women who work at home (a.k.a. the "mommy wars"). Serving the family is honorable work, and it is one of many ways God calls women to fulfill his purposes in the world. But also imagine how God could be glorified through the influence of an executive who makes her company a more caring, humane place to work. The dividing line between these forms of work has become blurrier as Christian women blend their gifts and responsibilities in response to the pressures of modern life. This integration of roles reflects a biblical model in which men and women labor together for the economic, social, and spiritual welfare of their families and communities.

In addition to affirming a wide range of roles, a broad view of the gospel invites us to see ourselves as stewards of our talents across various life stages. It's rare to find a woman whose career will follow an unwavering growth trajectory throughout her life. For this reason, we must develop *vocational imagination*—the ability to adapt and envision new ways for God to work through our vocation (from the Latin *vocatio*, "a response to God's voice")—as our circumstances change. Questions like, "God, how will you use me in *this place*?" or, "How are you leading me to use my skills and resources in *this season*?" require creative, flexible responses. Whether we are single professionals, parents juggling young children and part-time work, or soon-to-be empty nesters wondering what's next for our careers, we need a vision for women's work that is broad enough for the unique situations we face. We can rest in these transitions, knowing that God's primary call for women *and men* is the same—to follow him and fulfill his purposes in the world.

REFLECT

Consider your daily work with a broad view of the gospel in mind. What is broken or strained in your current workplace or its systems? Where do you see opportunities to infuse qualities such as God's goodness, beauty, or truth?

Examples:

An annual review process isn't effective or leaves employees feeling discouraged. A biblically inspired approach might balance grace and truth (see John 1:14) so that employees receive clear feedback about their performance with encouraging praise about ways they've excelled.

A teacher recognizes that her students bring complex personal issues into her classroom. While she can't change the social and cultural dynamics outside the school, she can create an atmosphere that reflects God's peace and unconditional love in her classroom.

3

Cultural Norms Versus Biblical Norms

Her husband has full confidence in her and lacks nothing of value. . . . She selects wool and flax and works with eager hands. . . . She provides food for her family. . . . She considers a field and buys it; out of her earnings she plants a vineyard. . . . She opens her arms to the poor and extends her hands to the needy. . . . She speaks with wisdom, and faithful instruction is on her tongue.

PROVERBS 31:11, 13, 15-16, 20, 26

Over the last decade, I have talked to hundreds of women about their calling, and in the process have discovered how complex perspectives about women and work can be. The factors shaping women's thinking about work are as unique as our fingerprints, formed by our family or ethnic background, personality and drive, relationship status, and church background. For this reason, it is critical to explore the various influences that have shaped *our* understanding of what it means to be a Christian woman.

Throughout the Bible, we see women working to meet the physical and financial needs of their families and communities. Proverbs 31, a model of godly productivity for both men and women, shows a woman engaged in commerce *and* childcare—an inspiring example for women with entrepreneurial and leadership gifts. In spite of this vibrant example of a woman who integrated her work as a craftswoman, landowner, and mother, well-meaning Christians may miss the complete vision God has for women and their work. This often happens when we divide work into private (home-based) and public (marketplace or civic) spheres.

This model of men and women working together in home-based labor, such as agriculture or the trades, existed for centuries until technological and economic changes altered the way people work. Beginning in the mid-1700s in the United Kingdom, the industrial revolution redefined economic production by moving work into factories. It was common for both men and women to work outside the home—until a couple became prosperous enough for the woman to stay home to care for their family. Instead of integrating economic production and family care, men and women began to occupy distinct spheres of influence. While men braved the rough, tough life of factories and city streets, women maintained the safety and moral goodness of the home. Historians refer to this period as the "Golden Age of Domesticity," as a woman's work maintaining a household was valued over other expressions of her calling.

In her book *Love Thy Body: Answering Hard Questions about Life and Sexuality*, Nancy Pearcey illustrates how societies operated prior to the industrial revolution and its aftereffects:

> In pre-industrial societies, most work was done on the family farm or in home industries, where husband and wife worked side by side. Women were involved in economically productive labor, while men were far more involved in raising and educating children than most are today. What changed all this was the Industrial Revolution. It took work out of the home—and that seemingly simple change dramatically altered gender roles. The result was greatly constricted roles for both men and women—which in turn led to narrower definitions of masculinity and femininity.[1]

The consequences of these historical and cultural trends affect many women today, especially those from White, evangelical backgrounds. Older millennials, and the women before them, may have been raised with the perspective that a woman's primary responsibility was to home and family. Melissa Russell, regional president of North America for the global nonprofit International Justice Mission (IJM), learned firsthand how hard it can be for women to integrate their roles as she rose to executive leadership. When she joined the staff at IJM, she knew she was called to organizational leadership, but she says, "For the first five to seven years, I felt a tremendous amount of guilt about it." As a White woman growing up in the southern United States, it was expected that once she had children, she wouldn't work outside the home. Melissa thought that God was just *enduring* her leadership and professional gifts, but through prayer, reading, and teaching, she felt God say to her, "I'm not [just] enduring your gifts; I gave you these gifts—on purpose, for a purpose. . . . These are things I have given you to use, in a way that helps bring order to chaos. . . . God wants us to take up the full place that he's given us. He does not want us to pull back from that. We don't bless anyone by leaving [our gifts] off the table."[2]

How does your experience compare to Melissa's? You may be less affected by cultural norms around stay-at-home motherhood. Financial realities or single parenthood may have made it unrealistic not to work outside the home, or you may have been raised by women who built compelling careers. These varied experiences remind us that to be biblical, our vision for women's roles must be accessible to any woman, in any stage of life or socioeconomic status, anywhere in the world, at any point in history. To imply that a single model represents a biblical ideal denies the diversity of the human experience—and the diverse roles we see women play in Scripture.

REFLECT

What influences have shaped your understanding of women's roles (such as where you live, your faith background, your unique family dynamics, your age)?

What emotions have surfaced as you seek to develop your gifts? What tension points do you encounter in your roles?

What It Means to Be Called

May God himself, the God of peace, sanctify you through
and through. May your whole spirit, soul and body be
kept blameless at the coming of our Lord Jesus Christ.
The one who calls you is faithful, and he will do it.

1 THESSALONIANS 5:23-24

Throughout this book we will refer to your *call*, but if you're like many Christians, you may have questions about what it means to be *called*.

- What's the difference between a *vocation* and a *call*?
- Does God have a specific calling for every person—and if so, how will I know what mine is?
- Will I have more than one calling in life?

Pursuing God's purposes for your life will lead you on a daily adventure with him, but this need not be as mysterious as you may have been led to believe.

To understand what *calling*, or *vocation*, means, let's start with the roots. Kate Harris, author of *Wonder Women: Navigating the Challenges of Motherhood, Calling, and Identity*, understands the difficulty of defining one's vocation well:

> Vocation is derived from the Latin word "vox" or "voice" (translated into Greek as "call") so we take the broadest view of things: Vocation is one's entire life lived in response to God's voice, God's call. . . . Our various occupations— those activities, efforts, relationships, and responsibilities that quite literally "occupy" us day-by-day and season-by-season comprise how we see and make sense of our unique vocation as it is lived into over a lifetime. Most of our chatter about vocation tends to devolve into a conversation about titles and roles, skills and contributions, jobs and careers. . . . While this is a sensible way to put expression to our various efforts and intentions, we should recognize these singular explanations never sufficiently account for the fullness of our complex identities made in the image of a complex Trinitarian God. . . . We don't want to grapple with the overwhelming dimensionality of our calling, so instead we apply language that helps us wrap our heads around it.[1]

As Harris explains, our call touches every facet of life and is discerned through an active relationship with God. The following principles offer further clarification about calling.

Calling is more general than it is specific. A common misconception about calling is that God has predetermined every detail of our lives and will tell us specifically what he wants us to do.[2] In Scripture we see heroes such as Moses, Jonah, and Mary receive specific, miraculous instructions from God, yet that experience is not the norm, nor should it be expected. Before God ever calls us to a specific role or relationship, he calls us to himself—to a relationship with him, to a life of discipleship, and to serve others. As author Os Guinness explains, "We are not called to do something or go somewhere; we are called to *Someone. We are not called first to special work but to God.* The key to answering the call is to be devoted to no one and to nothing above God himself."[3] If this is the only direction you receive, it is enough to fuel a meaningful life. We have the privilege and responsibility to cocreate our lives with God, seeking his guidance as we use discernment and imagination to make our way in the world.

Calling is usually **formed** *rather than* **found.**[4] You may think, *If God would just tell me what to do, then I would do it.* Instead, our call takes shape over time as he leads us through circumstances that strengthen and form our character. Like a block of marble that will become a sculpture, God gradually sculpts us into the shape that best serves the opportunities and relationships ahead. We may not see what the final form will be, but we can trust that each step or strike of God's chisel will form us according to his design. Our call often expresses itself in layered ways through our roles and relationships—you may be a spouse, an aunt, a citizen, and an employee.

Calling is not something that we passively wait to figure out. We can confidently explore opportunities, knowing that God will never leave us. Jesus reminded his disciples, "Surely I am with you always, to the very end of the age" (Matthew 28:20). This is an invitation to take steps forward as we trust, look, and see.

REFLECT

How is God's general call (to relationship with him, to a life of discipleship, to serve others) expressed in your life?

As you reflect on your life, how have you seen God prepare you over time for future opportunities? What might this reveal about your calling?

Tools to Explore Your Calling

*Calling provides the story line for our lives,
and thus a sense of continuity and coherence in
the midst of a fragmented and confusing modern world.*

OS GUINNESS

We live in a world addicted to choice. As author Os Guinness observes:

Life has become a smorgasbord with an endless array of dishes. And more important still, choice is no longer just a state of mind. Choice has become a value, a priority, a right. To be modern is to be addicted to choice and change . . . choice and change lead quickly to a sense of fragmentation, saturation, and overload. In the modern world there are simply too many choices, too many people to relate to, too much to do, too much to catch up with and follow, too much to buy. . . . At some point different to us all a cut-off switch kicks in. We are overloaded, saturated. There is too much to do and too little time to do it.[1]

Maybe you can relate. The pressure to keep up with family commitments, work responsibilities, and your online presence across various social media platforms can be exhausting. One of the beauties of calling is that it offers a through line, an invisible thread that binds your story together across the seasons and stages of your life. In chapter four we introduced the idea that calling is more general than specific: you are called to a relationship with God and his mission in the world before you are called to a specific place or role. This broad view of calling turns life into an adventure as you discern God's leading and use imagination and initiative to find effective ways to use your God-given gifts.

Yet the question remains: How do you respond to the innumerable choices life offers? For Katie Macc, the cofounder of the financial technology firm Juntos Global and chief operating officer at the Sorenson Impact Center, calling has led her through roles as diverse as running a microfinance program in Rwanda, to working with software engineers in Silicon Valley, to raising her preschool-aged son. Reflecting on how God has led her professional life, Katie sees repeated moments of *flare* and *focus*. The flare moments are when she tries new things that may not seem like a logical step in her career journey; the focus moments are ones when she concentrates her efforts on a proven process or objective. While her career journey is not linear, it is intentional, and it reveals a thread that God has used to unite the various stages. "Over time, those moments of flare and focus tell a story, a journey about who God is making me to be and how he's pulling me forward," she says.[2]

Katie offers three practices that have helped discern God's direction for her life:

Plot your journey. Reflect on the various stages of your educational or working life and note moments of flare and focus. If you're a visual learner, it may help to chart your path, noting significant stages or personal events. You might find that the times when you were "flaring" to try something new—such as moving to another state or taking a class on a topic you had always been interested in but never pursued—reveal possible avenues for focusing your efforts in the future.

Keep a "next" list. Start compiling a list of opportunities you would like to pursue in the future. Allow your imagination to roam as you list qualities or experiences you dream of achieving in your professional life. As a tall woman, Katie's list includes her desire to travel in the more roomy business class for work (she hasn't achieved that item yet) and to lead a team for which she has an opportunity to shape and cast vision. "Some of them may never come true, but it helps to keep them on a list to guide your efforts," she says.

Find a friend whose personal or professional journey resonates with yours. Identify someone who understands the complexities of your life and is invested in your success. Plan time to talk and dream about your professional growth, whether those conversations happen over coffee, quarterly phone calls, or annual getaways. This type of friend is essential to encourage, challenge, and hold you accountable to developing your gifts.

Living your call does not depend on God declaring a single, glorious vision for your life. Rather, it's a lifelong journey that combines spiritual discernment, courage, and creativity as God helps you become the woman he designed you to be. "I feel a very deep resonance with who God made me to be," reflects Katie Macc. "[As I walk closely with him], my call is to become fully alive and enable as many people around me to become as fully alive as possible. I see my work aligning with that, whether it's helping advance human flourishing or helping people do work in their daily lives that will make them feel more alive. The common thread of that is rooted in the gospel."

REFLECT

Name a flare moment you've had in your career—something new that you tried that did not follow your usual pattern. What did you learn by deviating from your norm?

Start building your "next" list. What is one practical goal and one aspirational goal you would like to accomplish?

Identify a friend who might help you dream about your professional development. Schedule a time to introduce the idea of supporting each other in this way.

PART TWO

Build Strength from Within

6

Identify Beliefs That Limit Your Growth

Do not conform to the pattern of this world, but be transformed by the renewing of your mind. Then you will be able to test and approve what God's will is—his good, pleasing, and perfect will.

ROMANS 12:2

Have you ever thought to yourself, *I'm no good at this! I'll never be able to meet this goal,* or *I don't have enough experience for this role.* If so, you've fallen prey to limiting beliefs, a common challenge women (and men) face in the workplace. Limiting beliefs are judgments about yourself or your abilities that keep you from working toward a goal. They can create anxiety, paralyze you, and keep you from growing into the woman God created you to be.

Limiting beliefs form from direct and indirect influences and lurk in the corners of your mind, whispering words of doubt or fear. Maybe your father joked about your intelligence, saying it's a good thing you were pretty because you'd need to advance through your looks. Or a guidance counselor questioned your decision to apply to a certain college, pointing you toward options that didn't match the scope of your ambition. These messages can sink into your mind, shaping how you see yourself and your potential.

The good news is that limiting beliefs can change if you understand their source and counter these false messages with biblical truth. Life coach Charlena Ortiz, founder of the women's empowerment network Grit & Virtue, understands these messages well, as she faces them in her own work. In an episode of the *Faith & Work Podcast*, she identifies common questions that cause people to doubt their abilities:

Am I enough? This question tends to appear when you take professional risks or embrace new challenges. Maybe a life change, such as becoming a mother, causes you to question how you will be able to get everything done.

Am I loved? Life experiences and upbringing can cause us to question our belovedness. We may agree intellectually that God loves us, but functionally we may act as if that is in doubt.

Do I have anything valuable to offer? This is a question that many women ask regarding their voice and influence. Maybe you don't feel as articulate as a coworker or you struggle to organize your thoughts when you're put on the spot in a meeting. Or maybe you're the only extrovert on a team of introverts and worry that your personality is "too much." If you absorb these messages, you may wonder if people will actually listen to what you have to say. When you question the value and authority of your words, you may hold back from taking risks or sharing a message that only you can deliver.[1]

If you have ever struggled with these questions, take heart, because you are not alone. Limiting beliefs plagued the lives of some of the most influential people in the Bible. In Exodus 3 and 4, God tells Moses that he is sending *him* to bring the Israelites out of Egypt. Moses' response is to ask, "Who am I?" Later, Moses tries to convince God that he's not the man for this job: "I have never been eloquent, neither in the past nor since you have spoken to your servant. I am slow of speech and tongue" (Exodus 4:10). In both instances, God reminds Moses that he will strengthen him for this role: "Who gave human beings their mouths? Who makes them deaf or mute? Who gives them sight or makes them blind? Is it not I, the LORD? Now go; I will help you speak and will teach you what to say" (Exodus 4:11-12).

Charlena offers the following practices to overcome your limiting beliefs:

Journal to increase your self-awareness. "When I sit down to journal, I'm not just recording my day, I'm processing it with the Father," she says. "[For] every emotion and every thought that comes up, I can invite him in to ask, 'Lord, what is it that you want me to know about you as it relates to the topic at hand?'"

Develop a biblically based identity statement. Even if a truth is hard for you to believe in the moment, it will bring you back to who you are in Christ. As a coach, Charlena uses this identity statement to guide her work with clients: *I am resourceful, creative, and whole. [Through Christ] I have what it takes to unlock the true beauty in women and to help set them free.* She's drafted different statements for other areas of her life, including her work as a business owner, mother, and wife.

Anticipate that limiting beliefs will appear as you work. When you feel anxiety, stress, fear, anger, or any emotion that seems outside your normal range, look inside yourself to identify the underlying belief fueling your response. Ask yourself, *What's really going on here? What is the worst thing that could happen in this situation? Am I anticipating trouble or trying to protect myself?* Training yourself to spot limiting beliefs will help you disarm them quickly.

Invite God into the process. Pop psychology relies on the power of positive thinking, which suggests that we have unlimited power within ourselves to change—if we believe strongly enough in our desired outcome. This way of thinking conflicts with biblical truth and puts the burden of change on our own shoulders. In contrast, true confidence combines biblical wisdom *with* human action. What a relief! God is ready to meet us with his truth and power, as Romans 12:2 reminds us. Through Christ, we are being transformed by the renewing of our minds.

REFLECT

Name a few beliefs that keep you from working with freedom and confidence.

Where do you think those beliefs come from? Did they come from loved ones or bullies or from how you've interpreted past experiences?

Write a biblically based identity statement for your work. Identify two situations in which you will be able to rely on this statement to boost your confidence.

God Grows Your Soul Through Work

I have calmed and quieted my soul,
like a weaned child with its mother;
like a weaned child is my soul within me.

PSALM 131:2 ESV

One of the best kept secrets of spiritual growth is the critical role your daily work plays in your development. Bible studies and time spent in prayer lay an essential foundation, but when the pressure is on in your job, it will force you to experience God in new ways. Just as the heat of a crucible burns off impurities to reveal pure silver or gold, the pressure you face as you live out your calling can produce radiant, mature faith. But how?

Work reveals the condition of your heart. Work invites you to examine your inner self—your motives, insecurities, temptations, or areas of discontent.

Work reveals areas for growth. Circumstances such as poor sales performance or frustrating interactions with your boss or clients can reveal sin in your life or ways in which you do not trust God.

Work reveals your need for God. Through self-examination, you will discover attachments—other than God—that capture your thoughts and affections. You will also see where you are striving or relying on your own efforts rather than abiding in God's peace and strength.

As circumstances reveal our spiritual condition, spiritual disciplines help us apply the gospel's truth to our hearts. These practices, also referred to as *soul care*, help us experience God's presence and power in the midst of daily life.

Mindy Caliguire, founder of Soul Care, an organization supporting people's spiritual health, and director of personal growth at Gloo, a tech company in Boulder, Colorado, learned these lessons the hard way. When she and her husband were church planters in the 1990s, her drivenness led to physical and spiritual exhaustion. Mindy experienced severe neurological issues that forced her to step back from her work—a time-out that revealed the true state of her soul. In spite of the overflowing religious activity, she had neglected to connect with God in her labor. "My head was full of very good theology," she explains, "but I had no rhetoric or rationale for why I needed to intentionally carve out time and space to care for my own soul in the midst of everything else."

Through this experience, Mindy discovered the importance of soul care, practices that focus on building a life deeply connected to God. In contrast to a soul that is exhausted from striving, she points to the metaphor of a weaned child, described in Psalm 131:2. Although the child no longer needs to nurse from its mother, it longs for her presence, much like our souls can long for God. As she explains, "[the verse] says: 'Like a weaned child is my soul within me.' There's nothing wrong with an unweaned child; [those babies are] just younger. They need to get something from the mother, so they come to her to *get*. A weaned child wants to hang out on its mother's lap [and] is there just for the sake of relationship."[1]

It's important to distinguish between spiritual practices—such as reading your Bible or attending church—and soul care. These practices lay an essential foundation for your faith, but they can become empty if not filled by your relationship with God. Soul care is about connecting with God's presence as he is *with* you and *for* you as you go about your work.

Rather than striving for purpose or satisfaction through your own efforts, a healthy soul overflows with hope, joy, and energy, and is able to maintain healthy emotional boundaries because it is rooted in God's strength. One way to cultivate a healthy soul is to converse with God throughout your day. You can rest in him moment by moment, crisis by crisis, decision by decision, and be reassured of his love, care, sovereignty, and goodness. Turn to him in the heat of the moment, like when your four-year-old is having a meltdown just before you have to make an important presentation on Zoom. "I don't see that as an invitation to muscle up to 'do what Jesus would do' at that moment, because I don't think anybody's willpower is that strong," Mindy explains. "[But] with the four-year-old screaming and the Zoom meeting starting, [we can] breathe in and be like, 'Okay, God. You're here. You're with me. You love this child. You're with this responsibility I am holding. How do you want me to navigate this moment? What do you want me to hear? Where is a solution that I'm not seeing right now? Open my eyes. Open my ears.'"

The beauty of connecting with God in a moment like that is that you can access his strength and rest in his presence whatever the circumstances. Give it a try! For a time, put aside practices that feel mechanical or lifeless, that don't result in you recognizing that you are loved by God. Pursue opportunities to connect with God, whether that means going for a walk or quietly listening for his voice in prayer. Notice what allows you to rest in God's presence and love for you.

REFLECT

God is *with you* and *for you*. How does knowing this make you feel about the challenges you face at work?

Think of a season in your life when your sense of connection with God was strong. How did that connection shape your spiritual life, your ability to navigate stressful situations, or the health of your relationships?

This week, experiment with a practice called *breath prayer*—simple phrases timed to the rhythm of your inhaling and exhaling. For example, the next time you feel stress at work, slow your breathing and pray one of the following prayers. Repeat the phrase five times, once with each breath in and out:

> Inhale: Nothing can separate me
> Exhale: From the love of God.
> Inhale: Jesus Christ / Exhale: have mercy on me, a sinner.
> Inhale: Be still / Exhale: and know that you are God.
> Inhale: Your grace / Exhale: is enough for me.

8

Cultivate Humble Confidence

Humility is not thinking less of yourself,
it's thinking of yourself less.

RICK WARREN

What is your personal brand? In the world in which you live and work, you have a brand whether you actively cultivate it or not. Your brand is your reputation. It's the impression you leave in writing, in personal interactions, and on social media. In the information age, it can feel like building a personal brand is essential to your success, but at times that can feel so self-promoting. The Bible commands us to "be completely humble and gentle" (Ephesians 4:2) and tells us that "God opposes the proud" (James 4:6). So how can women exude confidence in their work and leadership while demonstrating godly humility?

The internal conflict you feel balancing these divergent characteristics may come from misconceptions about what it means to be humble. To learn how to cultivate a humble confidence, let's begin by looking at what humility is not:

Humility is not insecurity. Jesus is described as being gentle and lowly of heart, but that lowliness and gentleness does not mean he was insecure. He was utterly clear about his purpose and was unwavering in that pursuit. It also helps that at the start of his public ministry (at his baptism) the Father declared, "This is my Son, whom I love; with him I am well pleased" (Matthew 3:17). That would fill anyone with confidence! Or think of the apostle Paul, who says, "By the grace of God I am what I am, and his grace toward me was not in vain" (1 Corinthians 15:10 ESV). There's a sense of clarity that although he was imperfect, God could work through Paul just as he was.

Humility is not indecisiveness. At times, we might think, *Well, if God wants it to happen, he will make it happen. And I don't have to do anything.* Yet in Genesis, God invites us to cocreate and develop the earth with him. He models proactivity through creation, then entrusts the world to us to release its potential. When you question your abilities, you're not bringing your best self to the work God has given you.

Humility is not passivity. God has equipped you with gifts to use, so being passive about your career is not humble or responsible. Your drive, when fueled by godly motivation and used in God-honoring ways, has the power to shape the world.

In contrast to these misconceptions, biblical humility is about living in agreement with what God says about you—it isn't arrogant or boastful, yet it's at peace with who God has made you to be. False humility, holding back, or diminishing yourself can hurt you at critical moments in your career, such as during the job search process. Because clearly stating your skills might feel like bragging, you may not share your strengths as boldly as you need to, even though the purpose of an interview is to demonstrate what you can accomplish. Humble confidence comes from knowing what is true of you: you are made in the image of God and he has given you specific strengths for the roles he intends you to fill. When you commit to stewarding the gifts God has given you, it frees you to excel, for God's glory and others' good.

Jena Viviano Dunay, a career strategist and founder of the Recruit the Employer Podcast, offers the following advice for Christians when developing their public presence or brand:[1]

Be honest about your motivation. Regarding social media, ask yourself, *Am I sharing this just to get likes or am I sharing this because I want to actually help people?* She admits there is pressure to keep up your personal brand, which may not be true to who you are. "It can err on the side of vanity, and we have to be really careful to not let it go that way," she advises.

Be careful not to center yourself in the process. "Even when my clients are worried about sounding humble, they're still just thinking about themselves, because they're worried about what somebody else [will] be thinking of them," Jena says. "At the end of the day, that's not really humble. That's still thinking 'What does everybody else think about me?' True humility is saying, 'Lord, I submit to what your plans are. I'm going to share the gifts you have given me. And if [I] don't move forward, I submit to that plan, because you have something else prepared for me.'"

Be willing to share knowledge. Confident, humble leaders display relational generosity. "I see a lot of people building their personal brands [who are] not willing to help people who are coming up behind them," Jena says. Be generous with your advice, your words, and your kindness toward other people who are less experienced than you.

REFLECT

How would you describe *humble confidence* in your own words? How is a Christian's confidence different from the confidence shown in popular culture?

How would others describe your personal brand? Ask a couple of trusted friends what words they would use to describe your reputation. What about that description shows humble confidence and what feels overly self-focused?

Think of an example from social media of someone with a personal brand who displays humble confidence. What is it about their postings that demonstrates humility?

9

Overcome Impostor Syndrome

Thank you for making me so wonderfully complex!
Your workmanship is marvelous—how well I know it.
You watched me as I was being formed in utter seclusion,
as I was woven together in the dark of the womb.

PSALM 139:14-15 NLT

Have you ever doubted your abilities? Hesitated to take advantage of a new opportunity or feared others would think you're unqualified? Maybe you feel like you don't fit in. If you've experienced any of these emotions, you're not alone! You're one of many women—from seasoned executives to middle managers to women just beginning their careers—who wrestle with self-doubt that can hinder their ability to lead. It's called *impostor syndrome*.

Psychologists Pauline Rose Clance and Suzanne Imes introduced the concept in a 1978 study that focused on high-achieving women. They observed that "despite out-standing academic and professional accomplishments, women who experience the impostor phenomenon persist in be-lieving that they are really not bright and have fooled anyone who thinks otherwise."[1] Research suggests that as many as 70 percent of people will experience impostor syndrome at least once in their lives. Once in their *lives*? If you've struggled with a season of self-doubt, you know it can be a daily or weekly occurrence when emotions are triggered by social media posts, critical feedback, or facing new challenges.

Entrepreneur and coach Merritt Onsa felt like an im-postor as she built her podcast, *Devoted Dreamers*. When it launched in 2016, she was content to interview other Christian women about their dreams, until her pastor asked her why she never spoke about her own dreams on the broadcast. Because Merritt was still figuring out how to host a podcast, she didn't feel she had anything to say and worried how her voice would be received. With great trepidation, she shared her first solo episode in 2018 and has continued to do so every month since. "Every time I think, [*What I have to say*] *is not very good*, I have to keep reminding myself that God made me for a reason. And two years later, people tell me that the solo episodes are their favorite ones. I hate that I keep having to get this affirmation externally, but it reminds me that it resonates with somebody when I show up." She encourages women to recognize that anytime they try something new or take a risk, they may face similar doubts. It's normal to feel discomfort in the midst of change; however, allowing the impostor syndrome to hold you back is "not listening to who God says we are, but who the enemy would accuse us of pretending to be."[2]

If you feel impostor syndrome creeping in, remember these points:

It's okay to make a mistake, but keep going. If you are pursuing something you are passionate about and skilled in, making a mistake doesn't mean you should stop doing the work for which God has gifted you. Recognize the voice of your inner critic and stop those lies before they affect you. Start looking for recurring themes so you can identify and resist false beliefs as they arise.

Ask for help as you pursue new skills. Collaborating with others doesn't mean that you are not equipped to do the work. Rather, it can set a supportive tone and encourage a growth mindset. As Carol Dweck, an expert on adult learning, explains, "Individuals who believe their talents can be developed (through hard work, good strategies, and input from others) have a growth mindset. They tend to achieve more than those with a more fixed mindset (those who believe their talents are innate gifts). This is because they worry less about looking smart and they put more energy into learning."[3]

Avoid leading with an apology or diminishing your ideas. How many times have you begun a statement with phrases like "I haven't researched this much . . ." or "I just want to add . . ."? Maybe you apologize for something that doesn't merit an apology saying, "Sorry to disagree." These can be difficult habits to break, so start by looking for ways you diminish yourself through your speech or writing. Don't minimize your authority unnecessarily! Plan ahead to lead with strong, positive messages throughout your work.

Let yourself stand out. Many women have told Merritt Onsa that when it comes to impostor syndrome, rejection is their ultimate fear. They allow themselves to fade into the background rather than stand out for their unique, valuable perspective.

Surround yourself with people who can affirm the gifts and abilities they see in you. You need people who can sort through false beliefs to help you see yourself and a situation clearly. These honest "rumblings," as sociologist Brené Brown calls the process of engaging shame, can stop impostor syndrome and move you toward positive action. Merritt adds, "If we are too fearful to try, no one ever gets the chance to open our eyes to the way that God made us." Doing so will allow you to call out strengths that you see in others who might be experiencing impostor syndrome too.

REFLECT

Think of a time when you experienced impostor syndrome. What helped you work through it?

Reflect on Psalm 139:14-15, quoted at the beginning of this chapter. How can remembering that God intentionally made you the way you are help you to combat impostor syndrome?

Do you have someone in your personal or professional network who affirms the gifts they see in you? What is one thing they have said that sticks with you?

Affirm someone else! What is a gift you see in another woman that you could call attention to?

10

Discover God's Gift of Rest

God appointed the Sabbath to remind us that
he is working and resting. To practice Sabbath is
a disciplined and faithful way to remember that
you are not the one who keeps the world running,
who provides for your family, not even the one who
keeps your work projects moving forward.

TIMOTHY KELLER AND
KATHERINE LEARY ALSDORF

If your home is anything like mine, it's typically a disaster by Friday night. The remnants of hurriedly eaten breakfasts crowd the kitchen counter, and a pile of workwear, thrown on a bedroom chair at the end of the day, has grown throughout the week. My mental and emotional state is no less cluttered, as lingering thoughts from a meeting compete with plans for my weekend activities. If some weeks it feels like your work never stops, you're not alone. "Work has fully invaded our personal lives in that we can work 24/7, but the reverse is not necessarily true," explains Christine Carter, PhD, a sociologist and senior fellow at the Greater Good Science Center at University of California, Berkeley. "We don't take our personal lives to work in the same ways that we are taking our work into our personal lives."[1]

While this may seem like a modern problem, God anticipated our tendency to overwork and designed sabbath as a solution. Through sabbath, soul-nourishing rest exists as a complement to good, God-given work, rather than as an escape from it. On the seventh day of creation, God rested from all his work (see Genesis 2:2) not because he was tired (Isaiah 40:28 says the Creator "will not grow tired or weary") but to enjoy what he had created. As God's image bearers, we work as he does, but we also rest, just as God did at creation. Pastor Tim Keller and marketplace ministry leader Katherine Leary Alsdorf explain:

> This rhythm of work and rest is not only for believers; it is for everyone, as part of our created nature. Overwork or underwork violates that nature and leads to breakdown. To rest is actually a way to enjoy and honor the goodness of God's creation and our own. To violate the rhythm of work and rest (in either direction) leads to chaos in our life and in the world around us. Sabbath is therefore a celebration of our design.[2]

Setting aside time away from work each week encourages us to shift our focus away from our toil to enjoy God and appreciate the fruits of our labor.

The Sabbath also declares our freedom from the burdens of work. In Deuteronomy 5:12-15, God commands the entire nation of Israel, who had just been released from slavery in Egypt, to rest one day a week. It's more than just a rule to be followed; the Sabbath was a fundamental principle that ordered the Israelites' lives. Imagine how they must have stood out from neighboring cultures by setting aside a day of rest every week, and how refreshing it must have been to rest after years of forced labor. Practicing the Sabbath reflected their distinct identity as God's people and modeled a flourishing way of life to a watching world.

To welcome the gift of sabbath rest, we must first wrestle with the outsized influence work has on our lives. As the Israelites knew, work can become a form of slavery. Anyone who cannot rest from work is a slave—to the need for success, to materialism, to the expectations of others, or to our employer's demands. Practicing sabbath also reveals the inner turmoil that keeps our souls from resting. You may be haunted by issues that underlie your work—the need to prove yourself, to gain a sense of worth and identity, or to avoid disappointing others. Finally, choosing to step away from work is an act of trust in God's provision. Will you lose the deal you've been chasing if you don't check your email on Saturday? What will your boss think of you if you aren't available 24-7? A sabbath practice encourages you to rest in Christ's finished work for your salvation (see Hebrews 4:1-10), not in your ability to save yourself.

Tara Owens, spiritual director and founder of Anam Cara Ministries, points out that God's "day six" of creation is humans' "day one." She explains:

> After six days, he stops. But for us humans, that was our first full day of existence, which says something really important about who God is, who we are, and who we are not. The pattern of creation, the one that we were intentionally placed into by God, is to start with stopping, to let our six days of work come out of rest. We take for granted the fact that God could have created human beings on any of the days of creation. Just maybe, the ordering of the days—of our days—matters a great deal to God, and to the ways God intends for us to go about our working and our stopping.

Owens goes on to say that the Sabbath is the very first thing in all of Scripture that God calls holy (in Hebrew, *kadosh*): "We think of God as holy, which he is, but before he even reveals himself as holy, he says that the Sabbath is holy. God says, 'I'm giving you this pattern of rest. The one I created in the beginning. Will you take me up on it?'"[3]

If you're intrigued by the idea of practicing sabbath, here are a few practical ways to plan a time of rest:

Make time for worship. Carve out alone time to reflect on your week and connect with God. This may take the form of corporate worship with your local church or through time alone in Scripture.

Pursue delight. Take a nap, enjoy a relaxing meal, do something recreational or creative that contrasts with what you do in your daily work. Tim Keller encourages people to do something "avocational" or unlike the things you do at work. For example, if you spend your days processing information at a desk, do something physical that gets you outside.

Unplug from technology. Seriously! You may feel removed from the outside world, but that's the goal—and the secret to true refreshment.

Recognize that various stages of life practice sabbath differently. Parents of young children may find it difficult to take twenty-four hours off from childcare duties, but you can strive to preserve the spirit of sabbath. For example, begin a habit of afternoon quiet time for the entire family or spend time playing together.

Prepare for your sabbath. A truly restful sabbath requires intentionality. Plan ahead to make the day special and to keep outside pressures from invading your time. Graciously clarify your availability to friends or colleagues.

REFLECT

Have you ever intentionally set aside time for sabbath rest? How did you structure your sabbath practice?

How could sabbath rest serve as a complement to your work rather than an escape from it?

What steps will you take to make sure the pressures of daily life don't creep into your sabbath? (For example, you could turn off email or social media notifications on your phone.)

What example of work/rest, delight, and trust would you like to set for your children, colleagues, or employees?

PART THREE

Navigate
Common
Workplace
Challenges

Lead with Authenticity and Intentionality

The most exhausting thing you can do is to be inauthentic.

ANNE MORROW LINDBERGH

Take a moment to envision what the ideal woman in your role or organization would be like:

- What is her educational or professional background?
- How does she dress?
- How does she communicate in meetings?
- Was she raised in a certain part of town?
- How do you measure up to that ideal?

One of the challenges of modern life is the volume of messages that suggest how we *should be* in almost every area of our lives. From how we diet or exercise, to how we parent, to the way we build our careers, there are innumerable ways we can change ourselves to live up to the ideal. It's tempting to adopt inauthentic tendencies to advance at work, yet research shows that's not the path to growth and satisfaction.

A 2008 study published in the *Journal of Counseling Psychology* found that authenticity (or "being true to oneself in most situations") produced higher self-esteem, lower stress, and greater satisfaction.[1] That's no surprise! When you compete against colleagues in self-serving ways, change yourself to fit in, or get caught in the pursuit of followers on social media, you will find yourself compromising who you truly are to succeed. Authenticity builds trust, and the more people trust you, the more true influence you will gain. But how can you stay true to yourself in spite of pressures at work?

Remember God's design. To be authentic, remember who made you and how you are made. Ephesians 2:10 teaches us: "We are God's handiwork, created in Christ Jesus to do good works, which God prepared in advance for us to do." The Greek word for *handiwork* (or *workmanship*) is *poiema,* which gives us our English words *poem* and *poetry.* It conveys the beautiful process of rebirth and re-creation that God began in our lives through Christ, a process that plays out in your life at work. Tim Keller captures the artistry of this process:

> Do you know what it means that you are God's workmanship? What is art? Art is beautiful, art is valuable, and art is an expression of the inner being of the

maker, of the artist. Imagine what that means. You're beautiful . . . you're valuable . . . and you're an expression of the very inner being of the Artist, the divine Artist, God Himself.[2]

To become inauthentic is to challenge the divine Artist's design.

Focus your energy. "It takes a lot of energy to be someone that you are not," Charisse Jones, founder of the coaching firm Grace + Grit Unlimited, explains. "But when you are who God made you to be, you can know with certainty that He is 100 percent behind you." When Charisse lost her job in 2020, she felt that God was giving her the opportunity to become a full-time entrepreneur. But before she launched her new endeavor, she asked herself, "Who is Charisse? What are my core values? What is my mission and how will I leverage this new authority God is giving me?" She developed a clear sense of who she was and what she was called to build for the kingdom of God. "When we are clear about what's important and what's of value, we can be intentional about where we invest time, focus, and energy."[3] Why spend emotional energy trying to be someone you're not?

Wear your own dreams. In 1 Samuel 17, we see the young shepherd David preparing to fight the enemy warrior Goliath. King Saul honored David by dressing him in his own tunic and armor—battle gear worthy of a king! Yet it didn't fit David's smaller body. Rather than enter the battle wearing someone else's idea of a warrior's garb, David chose clothing and weapons that fit: five smooth stones, a shepherd's bag, and his sling. This unlikely, undersized shepherd defeated the giant Goliath, and he did so by being true to himself.

Prepare to speak up. Don't leave something as important as how you will be perceived to chance. When do you feel the most pressure to diminish or change who you are? You know the situations that make you feel inadequate, so meet those lies with the truth of who God has made you to be.

REFLECT

What things or people do you tend to root your identity in rather than Christ? What have been the consequences of finding your identity outside of him?

Think of a time when you adopted someone else's lifestyle, expectations, or goals as your own. How did it feel to "wear" values that weren't your own?

In what moments do you feel the most pressure to compromise your true self? Identify two small steps you could take to anticipate those situations and to help you stay authentic.

12

Realize Your Vocational Power

The people who follow God's heart and ways see everything they have as gifts to be stewarded for his purposes.

TIMOTHY KELLER

Power. For many Christian women, the word is heavy with meaning related to their roles in marriage, church, and the world. Yet we long to feel more empowered, to know that our gifts are valued, and to influence others with confidence and strength. As followers of Christ, we are invited to wrestle with our relationship to power.

In the Gospel accounts of Christ's life, we marvel as he uses his power on behalf of women. Imagine how the woman who suffered from gynecological trouble (what some translations refer to as an "issue of blood") felt in Mark 5:29-30, when she grasped Jesus' clothes: "Immediately her bleeding stopped and she felt in her body that she was freed from her suffering. At once *Jesus realized that power had gone out from him.* He turned around in the crowd and asked, 'Who touched my clothes?'" (emphasis added). What must it have been like to feel the healing power of God in that moment? What might it have been like to stand with Martha at the tomb as Christ raised her brother, Lazarus, from the dead (see John 11) or with Mary as she encountered the resurrected Christ outside another empty tomb on Easter morning (see John 20)? Christ met each woman in her fear and despair with a demonstration of his power and love.

Christ continues to offer his power to his followers, as he strengthens us to love and serve a broken world. Many churches help their members discover tools, such as spiritual gifts, to steward this power but overlook vocational skills and resources that could be used to advance God's purposes. Your daily work is one of the most profound ways you can serve using God's power for his glory and others' good. It's time to get serious about using your vocational power!

God has placed you where you are and equipped you for his purposes. "That I am who I am is not a result of chance, a mere cosmic accident. Rather it is the result of God's intention," explains theologian Lee Hardy. "There is a reason why I am who I am, although that reason may not be immediately apparent to me. I was placed here for a purpose, and that

purpose is one in which I am, in part, to discover, not invent."[1]
Part of the discovery process Hardy refers to is learning to
steward the unique resources and opportunities God has
given you through your daily work. This vocational stewardship is the intentional, strategic deployment of your power,
knowledge, platform, networks, position, influence, skills, and
reputation, to advance God's kingdom. Your work today can
give a foretaste of the kingdom, a sample of what lies ahead,
as Christ prayed in Matthew 6:10, "Your kingdom come, your
will be done, on earth as it is in heaven."

What does it look like to help God's kingdom come through
our work, relationships, and resources? In her book *Kingdom
Calling: Vocational Stewardship for the Common Good*, scholar Amy
Sherman identifies seven forms of vocational power that can
be used for God's purposes.[2] As you read, consider which
forms of power you possess:

Knowledge/Expertise: Your education and training com-
bined with on-the-job experience. Since work intrinsically
matters to God, we have a duty to "serve the work" and strive
for professional excellence. Pursuing professional development opportunities will equip you to make an even greater
contribution through your daily work.

Platform: Your ability to get the message out by drawing attention to an issue, cause, person, place, or organization.
Stewarding your platform is a serious responsibility as it

requires a commitment to communicate the truth with accuracy and a regard for human dignity.

Networks: We all exist within relational networks that allow us to share resources and opportunities. God can advance the kingdom through your professional contacts, civic relationships, partnerships, and involvement in organizations.

Position: Your standing within an organization gives you certain rights and responsibilities. Holding a position of power offers specific privileges. However, even if you aren't at the top of an organization, you can manage the power you've been given through that role. Never underestimate the power middle managers have to shape people's lives.

Influence: You don't have to hold a formal leadership position to exert influence. Start by using the measure of influence you currently have and ask God for the courage to "lead up" by influencing those with greater power than you.

Skills: Making time to inventory your skills can open new avenues of service. Ask yourself, "For whom could I deploy these abilities?"

Reputation: Your name recognition can give access to power-brokers, the ability to mobilize large groups of people, or draw attention to a need. You are more powerful than you may realize. Use the reflection questions below to explore the power unique to your role and relationships.

REFLECT

Of the seven areas of vocational power identified by Amy Sherman, which three are most evident in your life?

What opportunities exist for you to use this power to serve a cause, your colleagues, or your community?

What steps can you take to strengthen these areas of power for even greater impact? This may mean pursuing additional training, collaborating with people who have other areas of power, or leading a conversation with like-minded friends to assess their vocational power.

13

Resist the Need to Be Perfect

But he said to me, "My grace is sufficient for you,
for my power is made perfect in weakness."
Therefore I will boast all the more gladly about
my weaknesses, so that Christ's power may rest on me.

2 CORINTHIANS 12:9

If you work in a competitive field or struggle with anxiety, you may have perfectionistic tendencies. Maybe you're a passionate, hard-driving worker who has unrealistic standards for yourself (and others). Whether you internalize other people's expectations or feel like your work is never done, perfectionism can keep you from thriving at work and living in the freedom and peace God offers.

A 2018 survey of almost five thousand corporate workers in Australia found that women struggled with perfectionism and self-criticism to a higher degree than men.[1] "When a professional endeavor goes wrong, women are more likely to blame themselves," explains journalist Jessica Bennett.

> Yet when something goes right, they credit circumstances—or other people—for their success. . . . Women are more likely than men to be perfectionists, holding themselves back from answering a question, applying for a new job, asking for a raise, until they're *absolutely 100 percent sure* we can predict an outcome. . . . We doubt our opinions and begin our sentences with, "I don't know if this is right, but—" We are more prone to "rumination" than men—which causes us to overthink and overanalyze. (Sound familiar?)[2]

Although common, perfectionism will rob the joy from work and can have long-term negative effects on your life.

THE COSTS OF PERFECTIONISM

It causes burnout. When good is never good enough, you will overwork to the point of exhaustion even though, on this side of heaven, perfection is not achievable. Jo Saxton, a leadership coach and author of *Ready to Rise: Own Your Voice, Gather Your Community, Step into Your Influence,* has seen it many times: "[When we believe that] everything has to be perfect, and we keep on absorbing all the roles . . . all the roles . . . all the roles . . . and being excellent at them all, it burns us out, not surprisingly. Because no one person is designed to do that."[3]

It hinders collaboration. Perfectionism locks us inside ourselves and limits the scope of our impact to what we can control. It blinds us from seeing how we lead and grow through a circle of relationships. "One of the things we don't often recognize is that leadership has always happened in community," Saxton says. "One of my friends often describes women leaders like orphans. They don't know how to 'parent' anybody else because they didn't encounter it themselves. They're like, 'I'm not actually sure how I even got here. All I can tell you is, work like crazy and maybe you, too, will get here.' We have to thoroughly dismantle [this idea]. You have to break up with the overachievement addiction to be able to move forward." Imagine how your insight and experience could bless younger leaders if you had the emotional energy to invest in these relationships.

It keeps you from loving your neighbor. Sometimes women can be unkind or unsupportive to their female colleagues. With fewer women in leadership, it's easy to operate with a scarcity mindset or expect women to "pay their dues" on the way to the top. "I've seen it again and again," says Saxton. "You see how popular [a new female colleague] is with people from whom you have worked hard for years to gain respect. You think, *I've worked hard for this. I've sacrificed for this. I've been patronized for this.* There is a buildup of resentment because of the thousand cuts to the heart [you've experienced]. The whole thing about breaking through the glass ceiling is that you still get cut by glass. So when [younger colleagues] walk in [more easily], some people aren't always happy about it."[4]

HOPE FOR OUR PERFECTIONISM

How can you find relief from perfectionistic tendencies?

Begin by recognizing perfectionism as a lie. Perfectionism is rooted in the belief that we can earn love or work our way toward being accepted. It feeds on the unrealistic idea that we can control the outcome of our lives by living up to an elusive ideal. Rooting out these deeply held beliefs may require the help of a qualified counselor or spiritual director.

Remind yourself that the perfect is often the enemy of the good. Perfectionism is a pride-based or fear-based compulsion that can paralyze you and cause you to neglect what is necessary and good. It will trap you in a cycle of never-perfect projects instead of allowing you to pursue new opportunities and a broader scope of work.

Soak your life in Scripture that reminds you of God's perfection and love for you. The author of Hebrews teaches us, "For by a single offering [Jesus] has perfected for all time those who are being sanctified" (Hebrews 10:14 ESV), while the apostle Peter reminds us of our identity in Christ: "But you are a chosen people, a royal priesthood, a holy nation, God's special possession, that you may declare the praises of him who called you out of darkness into his wonderful light" (1 Peter 2:9).

And Jesus invites us to share the weight of our imperfection with him, saying, "Come to me, all you who are weary and burdened, and I will give you rest. Take my yoke upon you and learn from me, for I am gentle and humble in heart, and you will find rest for your souls. For my yoke is easy and my burden is light" (Matthew 11:28-30).

Overcoming the need to be perfect will take gradual, sustained effort, but it is possible with God's help. He loves you too much to let your life—and your potential—be limited by lies.

REFLECT

Is there an area of your life where you notice more perfectionistic tendencies—at work, at home, or with your family? Why do you think this is?

Can you recognize the voice of your inner critic? What messages does it send that weaken your confidence?

Think of a time when you allowed yourself to be vulnerable and it helped a personal situation, work project, friendship, or relationship with a colleague? How did showing vulnerability affect the relationship?

14

Lead Up

Early in my career, I found myself in some situations
where just because of my closeness to the ground,
I could see details that a leader above me couldn't see.
I was able to lead—not from a position of authority—
but from a perspective that would really benefit leadership.
It's another way to promote human flourishing,
and help the world become something that
is the way God would want it to be.

BRIAN GRAY

At our annual Women, Work & Calling conference, some
attendees say they struggle with their lack of authority in their
organizations. In contrast to the executives and founders they
see on stage, how much influence do they have when they
work in the middle of a large corporation? More than you
might think! In management terms, the idea of leading from
the middle is called "leading up." Because leading up is a

learned skill, mastering it can empower you to exert influence in any role. The challenge is learning how to exert this influence effectively and in a godly way.

No matter what your role is, you have opportunities to lead up as you engage the individuals or groups who have authority over you. Your input matters because you may see details or perspectives that your leader may not be able to see. However, expressing your observations in a way that adds to a team's shared knowledge, rather than competing with your leader's authority, can be tricky. As leadership guru John Maxwell says, "Most leaders don't necessarily want to be led." They do, however, want value added to what they're doing. Here are some tips for respectfully sharing your perspective.

Make sure your heart is in the right place. As Christians, leadership is a stewardship opportunity. We steward our gifts, our perspective, our emotional intelligence, our access to data, and our institutional history on behalf of the mission. When done well, leading up serves the broader purpose of your organization. Just make sure that you're not trying to push your own agenda. Pray through the decision to speak up. Ask yourself, "Am I only bringing this up because it's the way I want it done, or will this really benefit the staff, community, or organization?"

Strive for continuous improvement any time you lead up. Emphasize that you chose to voice your concerns because you care about your company's clients, products, or employees.

Consider your timing and tone. In the book of Esther, we see that Esther took the timing and tone seriously when she approached King Xerxes to plead for the lives of the Jewish people. Esther first asked the Jews to fast for three days before she approached the king. Then she invited the king to a banquet, and after two days of feasting, she made her case—all the while knowing she could be killed. In the end, Esther's courage saved the lives of her people. This is leading up at its finest.

In today's work culture, considering your timing and tone will increase the likelihood that you'll be heard. Recognize your leader's meeting rhythms and stressful seasons, and time your request to the organizational calendar. The worst time to request additional funding is shortly after the annual budget is finalized. Understand that if your boss is in the middle of meeting a monthly deadline or quarterly financial goal, his or her availability and mental capacity to discuss big-picture goals might be limited.

Consider the communication method that best suits the suggestion you have. If it's a quick idea, using Slack or sending a text might be best. If you predict that a longer discussion will be necessary, ask to go for a walk or schedule an in-person meeting, depending on your manager's preferences.

If your manager has an administrative assistant, talk to that person about the scope and purpose of what you want to discuss. It might be easier for your manager to absorb an idea if they've received a brief summary from their admin before the meeting.

Be solutions oriented. It's easy to notice mistakes and what goes wrong, but it takes more skill to look beyond the problems to figure out what to do next. A boss does not want to hear what didn't work; they may already know. Offer right-sized solutions that could solve the problem moving forward. And present your ideas with a positive, forward-looking attitude.

Doing so can also increase your influence. It might not change your position, but it will change how others perceive your value. Over time, this can increase the God-centered influence you have in your day-to-day work.

Seek to understand others' jobs. Recognize the range of pressures your managers face that exceed the burdens you carry in your own role. Have compassion and empathy for people whose responsibilities differ from your own. Hopefully, they'll do the same for you, as you collaborate on a shared mission.

REFLECT

Think of a time when you approached a leader about a problem you observed and it wasn't well-received. Why do you think the leader responded that way?

In contrast, think of a time you approached a boss about an issue and it was well-received. What factors contributed to a more receptive response?

Think practically. How could you apply one of the principles of leading up to your current workplace?

Be Aware of
the Double Bind

*One of the criticisms I have faced over the years is that
I am not aggressive enough, or assertive enough,
or maybe somehow because I am empathetic,
I am weak. I totally rebel against that. I refuse to believe
that you cannot be both compassionate and strong.*

**JACINDA ARDERN,
FORMER PRIME MINISTER OF NEW ZEALAND**

Relational. Nurturing. Caring. Studies show that people most often associate these qualities with adult women—and less often with adult men. Research also shows that people with these traits make great managers. What's confusing is that women in leadership are consistently rated as less successful managers. This disconnect between perceived and actual leadership effectiveness is referred to as the "double bind," a subtle but powerful dynamic that suggests women can be regarded as competent or likable, but not both. "It's an uphill struggle, to be judged both a good woman and a good leader," says Rosabeth Moss Kanter, a Harvard Business School professor who is an expert on women in leadership.[1]

Research suggests that men (whose leadership style is often described as "assertive" or "decisive") get a benefit from acting outside their gender stereotype, while women do not. When women display assertive or task-oriented traits—what could be described as taking charge—people tend to think, *I don't really like her.* But when women act more relationally and nurturing— actions that show a woman taking care—people tend to think, *I like her, but I don't think she will be a strong leader.* In contrast, when a man acts nurturing, outside expected gender norms, he's viewed positively by society.

Professor Deborah Streeter of Cornell University's SC Johnson College of Business explains it this way:

> The double bind means that women operate in a set of narrow boundaries. If they are too assertive, they are seen as aggressive and unlikable, but if they have care-taking qualities, that's affiliated with weakness. So women can't exercise the masculine behaviors of leadership as openly as men can. I sometimes call it the Niceness Penalty. Nice is not associated with power, it's associated with connectedness, which you need to be a strong leader. But you also need power. And that's

where women are stuck with this penalty [that] if you're too nice, you're not powerful. If you're not nice, people don't like you.[2]

If you find yourself caught in a double bind situation, what can you do?

Reflect on the example set by Christ. His life reflects moments of great tenderness (welcoming children, grieving with friends who lost a loved one), directive action (healing a demon possessed man, calming the sea), and moral outrage (overturning money changers' tables in the temple). This ideal man, the Son of God, was able to hold these seemingly conflicting characteristics in tension as he loved others and accomplished God's purposes. Pray for Christ's wisdom as you feel similar tensions.

Examine how your personality and gifts show up at work. Watch yourself in team interactions—do you tend to take charge of situations or take care of the people involved? Study a personality assessment like the Myers-Briggs Type Indicator, Enneagram, or StrengthsFinder (now CliftonStrengths). Do the qualities you display play into gendered stereotypes?

Look for opportunities to work against your type. For example, if you tend to be very collaborative and strive for consensus (often viewed as more feminine attributes) seize opportunities to display more decisive, "take charge" behavior. We're not suggesting you adopt a fake persona at work. Rather, look for opportunities to present a more well-rounded version of yourself.

Make sure your accomplishments are measurable and visible. Seek tangible ways to show your competence, using metrics of success that matter to the people in power. Relying on clear criteria not based on gender stereotypes will cut through bias and make a case for your impact. In addition, recruit the help of mentors or advocates who can amplify your accomplishments. Help them emphasize your competence through something like a "cheat sheet" that communicates your impact in quantitative terms. For example, you might create a chart showing how your sales numbers exceeded those of your peers or the improvements in educational outcomes students made through your teaching.

Engaging the double bind in thoughtful, intentional ways is not only good for your career. It can broaden your organization's understanding of effective leadership and make space for other gifted women to lead.

REFLECT

Have you ever experienced the double bind as a working woman? In what way?

What is an area of unconscious bias that you might have about masculine or feminine leadership styles?

From the list above, what is one step you could take to help present a well-rounded example of your influence at work?

PART FOUR

Pursue Purposeful Relationships

16

Re-envision Mentorship

My baseline definition of mentoring is this: mentoring is a relational practice, in which there's intentional pursuit towards growth and transformation.

LAURA FLANDERS

One of the keys to your development is building a network of relationships that encourage learning and professional growth. Sometimes referred to as mentoring, knowing how to find these strategic relationships has often been a struggle for career women. Many reasons keep us from these important connections; for some, it may be a lack of clarity about how to identify and ask a person for their time, while for others, the tendency of senior male leaders to invest in other men, who outnumber female leaders in the corporate sector, limits women's access to these relationships.

The good news is that mentoring is more accessible than you realize. Broadening your understanding of what it means to be mentored and building a constellation of learning relationships can enrich and advance your work. In this chapter, we tackle the top questions related to the purpose and process of mentoring.

What is mentoring? John C. Crosby, founder of the Uncommon Individual Foundation, says "Mentoring is a brain to pick, an ear to listen, and a push in the right direction." Notice how simple, yet broad, this definition is. It allows you to gain insight from a wide range of people, and it frees you from the pressure of finding an ideal mentor to meet your needs.

What should you look for in a mentor? Rather than looking for a single person to develop you, envision gathering a constellation of individuals who support you for various purposes and seasons of your life. Using John Crosby's definition, a mentor might be an experienced businesswoman who advised you in the early stages of your career, a neighbor lady who offered a wise, nonparental presence in your teen years, or the male boss who nudged you to apply for a position at another company when you outgrew your role. In each of these scenarios, the mentoring is relational, intentional, and encourages growth.

Stephanie Summers, CEO of the Center for Public Justice in Washington, DC, believes a false narrative exists that you should look for a mentor who is "the one." "I don't see a lot of support for that in Scripture, but I do see a lot of support for the distribution of gifts among the body. I think that frees us to ask people to share what God has given them," she says.[1] For years, Summers has asked people to share their insight in such a way that they may not realize they are mentoring her. She asks leaders for one hour of their time, in a place of their convenience, to discuss a specific challenge she's facing. Notice that she's not asking them to "mentor" her—she's only asking for their input. When they meet, she finishes the conversation by thanking them and repeating three things she learned during their conversation. Then Stephanie asks, in an open-ended way, if they would be willing to meet again. Ninety-nine percent of the time, even with people at the top of their fields, the answer is yes. "The more authentic leaders they are, the more generous they are to do that kind of thing," she says. Summers, in turn, does the same for others who wish to learn from her.

What's the role of the mentee? To answer this question, Laura Flanders, former mentoring director at Denver Seminary, points us to Christ. "He's a perfect model of being a learner, [a] perfect model of being a disciple. He is a perfect model of being a discipler, too, but I think we have to start with the reality that it says in Luke 2:52 that he grew in wisdom and stature. Our Christology is at play here. What does it mean for Jesus to be a fully human person? Well, it means that he developed, and he placed himself in a humble position to learn and to grow."[2]

"Then, later on in Hebrews 5:8-10, it indicates that he had to learn obedience," Laura explains. "It refers to the suffering he had to endure in his earthly life in order to learn obedience so that he could have empathy and compassion toward others. To learn that, he needed to go through suffering. I think that motivates me more than any example. To look at Jesus as a human person, and to say that he even entered into the life of being a mentee, and to being a learner and a grower. He had things to understand, even though he was without sin, and he was tempted like we are tempted. Through his humanity, he experienced many of the same things that we experience."[3]

Practically speaking, mentees need to be active participants in the learning process. Their engagement and willingness to learn, rather than passively expecting a mentor to bring all the insight, honors their mentor's time.

What about men and women mentoring each other? Denise Daniels, professor of entrepreneurship at Wheaton College, explains the benefits and complications of male-female mentoring: "Women will lack opportunities for mentoring and networking that their male counterparts might have [if] the guy can go to lunch with the boss, but the woman cannot. I've had wonderful male mentors who have been totally appropriate in the workplace, and I would not be where I am today were it not for those men."[4] To make mentoring opportunities available—and appropriate—for women, Denise suggests meeting with mentees in pairs or meeting in public places with visible sight lines. This strategy allows leaders, regardless of gender, to meet with men and women in the same fashion so that all colleagues can flourish equally.

Re-envisioning the mentoring process can open a world of new relationships to you. Who would you like to learn from next?

REFLECT

Who is one person you'd like to ask for an hour of their time to advise you on a specific topic?

Think about people you could mentor informally. How would you invite them to spend time with you?

If mentoring is a "brain to pick, an ear to listen, and a push in the right direction," which of these best describes what you could bring to a mentoring relationship?

17

Network in New Ways

*When we start to see people as the breadth of the gifts
that God has given them, rather than as transactions,
I think that is the "reframe" that networking needs.*

STEPHANIE SUMMERS

LinkedIn data shows that US women are 28 percent less likely than men to have strong professional relationships, a "gender network gap" that holds true around the globe.[1] A weaker network means that women may lack access to job opportunities, as a survey by Performance-based Hiring found that 85 percent of jobs are filled by networking[2]. In addition, women who lack strong relational connections may advance more slowly in their careers than their male counterparts. While this relational imbalance shapes women's working lives, it has profound spiritual implications too. When Christian women encounter barriers to growing their influence and resources, their gifts will be less broadly distributed in the world.

The question of why women have weaker professional networks baffles me, because I know many women who excel at developing relationships. But Makisha Boothe, founder of Sistahbiz Global Network, a business accelerator for Black female entrepreneurs, sees the situation differently: "I don't think we are bad at networking. I just don't think the system was built for us. I think we live in a patriarchal society where the system was built for the people who were running it at the time. Everything that we were raised to do was not built for that system, but for the other roles that we play in society."[3]

Instead of trying to assimilate to an old approach to networking, we can reframe the process to create relational networks in which a broader range of people are empowered to share their God-given talents with the world. Here are a few principles to shape a new approach to networking.

Start your day by praying for your relationships. Sarah Lampard, founder and CEO of AValue Insurance, encourages women to start the day anticipating the connections they will make, while also considering the eternal significance those connections could have. Pray something like, "God, lead me to the people that need me, and lead me to those that I need, also."[4] Makisha Boothe adds, "After you say the prayer, when you walk into a room, know that God has answered that prayer. Look at every person in that room as a person God has sent for a reason."[5]

Become softer. Stephanie Summers recalls times when, as the only woman on an executive team, she couldn't connect socially with her colleagues in the same way they did with one another. Once she watched the team stand outside a gathering, drinking Scotch and smoking cigars, in a group to which she wasn't invited. She thought, *This is not how Jesus wants these circles to be. Our pursuit of Christ is a relational circle, in which Christ is the center—not one in which any team member should be on the outside.* Summers used the experience to become softer instead of hardened, and she recognized that the people in that circle didn't know how they were affecting the women with whom they worked. "People's lack of competence is a fixable problem," she says. "So how do you help them know [that they're excluding people]? Then *they* have to be the ones to choose what they do with that [knowledge]."[6]

Encourage mutually beneficial relationships. A powerful misconception about networking is that we do it to accomplish our own goals—to land a promotion, connect with a potential client, or climb the social ladder. When regarded through the lens of faith, we build relationships to serve as Christ served us. As Philippians 2:3-7 reminds us:

> Do nothing out of selfish ambition or vain conceit. Rather, in humility value others above yourselves, not looking to your own interests but each of you to the interests of the others.

In your relationships with one another, have the same mindset as Christ Jesus:

> Who, being in very nature God,
>   did not consider equality with God something to
>   be used to his own advantage;
> rather, he made himself nothing
>   by taking the very nature of a servant.

In addition to approaching relationships with the right intentions, asking a new contact, "How can I best support your goals?" or "How can our organization encourage you in your work?" communicates your commitment to their good.

Stop the comparison cycle. Tattoo the words of actor and comedian Amy Poehler on your heart: "Good for her, not for me."[7] To truly support each other as we pursue our callings, we must curb a culture of comparison that can poison our relational networks. When Makisha Boothe started her business, she developed operating agreements that were intended to build a culture of support. "When a Black woman speaks, we listen" is one of her company's agreements, based on data that shows the opinions of Black women are often dismissed. "So when you are in this space, you are heard. We stand up for each other. We refer business to each other," she says. Makisha cultivates a work culture in which people remember that they are stronger when they work together. "When you find the courage to speak up on behalf of someone else when it is not popular," Boothe says, "I think that is the ultimate form of service."

REFLECT

How would you describe previous experiences you've had with networking?

Think of one or two women in each of the following categories and identify one simple step you can take to encourage them in their work:

- A colleague within your organization or existing relational network

- A competitor (or perceived competitor)

- A younger woman in the early stages of her career

18

Become a Relationally Generous Woman

Becoming relationally generous is good for our souls, yes, but it's also good for our business, and good for our leadership, and good for leaving a legacy of healthy leadership for men and women.

JO SAXTON

Have you ever caught yourself feeling competitive toward another woman in a professional context? (A better question may be, *When* was the last time you felt competitive toward another woman in regard to your work?) Maybe the two of you applied for the same promotion, a role in which few women have served, or maybe you're a small business owner whose competitor just unveiled gorgeous new branding, the type of improvements you'd like to make for your company but can't afford.

It's easy to allow these emotions to change how we work, making us believe there are limited resources available or causing us to grasp what we feel we need to succeed. However, like many aspects of the Christian life, God invites us to move away from our selfish tendencies to embrace generosity—relational generosity.

Women's leadership expert Jo Saxton likens operating from a scarcity mentality to playing a game of musical chairs. "You are running around the proverbial table, and there is only room for one or two of you. But there are forty of you running," she explains. "And all you can do is run as fast as you can and try to be in the right spot when the music stops. You do the dance of working twice as hard . . . trying to look right . . . trying to not be too argumentative . . . trying to act like you're useful. [You do] all of these things, so that when the music stops, hopefully you're the one who gets the job."[1]

She urges women to stop playing this game and instead make room in your networks for more women to contribute. As you seek to move from scarcity to generosity, the following principles can guide your relationships:

Call attention to other women's accomplishments. When we see examples of women serving in positions of influence, it illustrates what is possible for others. For a series of Instagram posts, Saxton chose to highlight the stories of women in the Bible. "I had a number of people DM me and say, 'Are these women real?' because they'd never heard them spoken of at church.

Others said, 'It's really frustrating to realize that there were women like me. There's Lydia, a businesswoman [see Acts 16], and there's Deborah who was a judge [see Judges 4–5] and I've never heard their stories.'" The lack of examples of women leading, especially for women in Christian circles, "has consequences in terms of what someone perceives is available [to them]," Saxton says. "Language creates culture. And it's worth thinking of what we've inadvertently created." What woman's work, in your circles, deserves recognition?

Amplify others' voices. Female leaders in the Obama administration caused a stir when they began to support one another's ideas in meetings.

> Female staffers adopted a meeting strategy they called "amplification": When a woman made a key point, other women would repeat it, giving credit to its author. This forced the men in the room to recognize the contribution —and denied them the chance to claim the idea as their own. "We just started doing it, and made a purpose of doing it. It was an everyday thing," said one former Obama aide who requested anonymity to speak frankly. Obama noticed, and began calling more often on women and junior aides.[2]

This is one example of women supporting one another to help their ideas be heard, but opportunities to make space for a range of perspectives to be heard at work abound.

Open your relational circles. Ask yourself what pathways you have created to help other women succeed. Do the women you want to see flourish get to be in the room when decisions are made? If someone doesn't play golf or enjoy a specific leisure activity outside the office, how will they get the same level of connection and networking opportunities as those who do participate in those things? Make a habit of connecting people who would benefit from knowing each other, but email each party involved to ask if they're open to being introduced before making the connection. That's good manners! A woman may not have space in her life to welcome a new connection, and introducing before asking can put one or both parties in the awkward position of saying no.

Share your power and resources. If you are a leader, offering opportunities to others may mean giving away what you have. When Jo Saxton was working in ministry, she remembers a time when she told her pastor she was tired of being the only woman in the room. Her pastor used his network to find a female leader that she could spend time with. He knew there were things that Saxton needed to learn from someone else, and he shared his relational network to find a person who could invest in her. "[People] will recognize that you were somebody who was secure enough and was intentional enough and saw [another person's] potential enough that you would leverage your networks to make sure they had access to the kind of leaders that would bring back something for your team," she says.[3]

Growing in relational generosity begins with recognizing the wealth of resources you already possess. Refer back to the discussion of "vocational power" in chapter twelve to remind yourself of what you have that could be shared with others.

REFLECT

When have you benefited from another person's relational generosity?

Spend a few minutes brainstorming a list of resources, relationships, or influence that you could share with another woman. Think of two people who would benefit from what you have to offer and make a plan to reach out to them in the next month to offer your support.

19

Restore the Blessed Alliance

Male-female relationships are to be a glowing testament to the fact that we are followers of Jesus.

CAROLYN CUSTIS JAMES

Men and women work side by side, wrestling with the same business challenges, attending the same meetings, and walking the same hallways. As we've explored throughout this book, we may be at odds with one another in the workplace. You may run across women who refer to their industry or workplace as an "old boys' club" or may feel worn down from working in a male-dominated setting. It can be challenging to learn to work together, just as it might be challenging for a man to work in a largely feminine context. Yet God, in his grand design for the world, made men and women to work together.

Author Carolyn Custis James describes the partnership God intends for men and women to form a "Blessed Alliance":

What has the ring of something innovative and progressive is actually a remnant of humanity's forgotten ancient past—an idea with primordial biblical roots that can be traced back to the Garden of Eden.

The notion that things work better and human beings become their best selves when men and women work together is found on page 1 of the Bible. When God was launching the most ambitious enterprise the world has ever known, the team he put together to do the job was male and female.

Adam and Eve faced a challenge of Mount Everest proportions that required a solid connection between themselves and their Creator. As His vice-regents, together they were charged with looking after things on His behalf—wisely to steward and utilize the earth's resources. Their goal together was to build His gracious kingdom on earth. No square inch of Earth is excluded. The arena of life is beyond the parameters of their joint rule. . . .

[God created a] Blessed Alliance between male and female. Having created his male and female image bearers, "God blessed them," then spread before them the global mandate to rule and subdue on His behalf.

According to Genesis, male/female relationships are a kingdom strategy—designed to be an unstoppable force for good in the world.[1]

It's common to assume this Blessed Alliance refers to the marriage relationship, but to do so ignores dynamic male-female partnerships seen throughout the Bible. Consider the examples of Esther and Mordecai, who saved the Israelites from a genocidal king; Aquila and Priscilla, who labored as tentmakers alongside Paul; or Mary Magdalene, Joanna, and Susanna, who funded Christ's ministry. The alliance also flows through church history in the work of Teresa of Ávila and John of the Cross, friends whose passion for Christ inspired Catholic renewal in sixteenth-century Spain, and William Wilberforce and Hannah More, whose leadership of the Clapham Circle helped abolish slavery in nineteenth-century England. Many of these partnerships existed in ministry contexts, but Wilberforce and More offer a glimpse of influence in public life.

By losing our vision for the Blessed Alliance, we've allowed the enemy to diminish our collective impact. We compete rather than collaborate, and as the #MeToo movement has shown, abuse those God intends as allies. At Denver Institute, we believe in a big gospel—the idea that Christ's death and resurrection restores not only individual lives but every corner of creation from the ravages of sin (see Colossians 1:19-20).

What might this big gospel mean for our professional relationships? Could reclaiming the Blessed Alliance yield partnerships that only the work of Jesus could explain?

As Carolyn Custis James argues, redeeming male-female partnerships is a powerful apologetic in a culture coming to terms with the scope of #MeToo: "God's original vision—a vision he has never abandoned but revives in the work of his son—was for relationships between men and women to be dazzling points of life on this spinning globe. Dynamics between men and women were never intended to be a battle of the sexes or a heated debate within Christian circles."[2]

To suggest that a short chapter of this book could solve difficult gender dynamics in the workplace, church, or community is shortsighted, nor does it encompass the unique culture of each group. But let this conversation begin a process that could produce lasting, life-giving change.

It starts with awareness and attitude. Do you need to confess a critical attitude regarding your male colleagues or leaders? It's easy to let frustration or painful experiences become a default negative attitude toward men. Eliminating gendered criticisms like "the old boys' club" is one way to start.

Look for conversation partners. Which men in your workplace or social circle would be open to exploring this theme with you? You need men to learn with and to highlight blind spots and biases of your own.

Pray for the Lord to heal and renew your perspective. Ask the Lord for a fresh vision of how he could work through stronger partnerships in your workplace or community. Ask him to lead you to divine appointments with men who share a similar desire to restore strained relationships between men and women.

REFLECT

Where have you seen glimpses of the Blessed Alliance in your daily life? What situations reveal how male-female collaboration is strained?

Take a moment to pray through the themes in this lesson. Ask God to reveal areas in which you need to grow. Ask him to lead you to trustworthy men who desire to restore the Blessed Alliance.

20

Don't Lean In,
Lean Hard

Cast your burden on the LORD, and he will sustain you.

PSALM 55:22 ESV

What comes to mind when you hear the term *lean in?* When Facebook COO Sheryl Sandberg published *Lean In: Women, Work, and the Will to Lead* in 2013, it became a clarion call for working women to engage their careers, especially in seasons when they'd be tempted to reduce their professional involvement. But over time, cracks began to show in Sandberg's argument. The mantra of ambition and hard work didn't account for the challenges of juggling caretaking and professional roles, especially for women who could not afford help to manage their households. As one journalist, who formerly ascribed to the "lean in" philosophy, observed, "Not only did my *Lean In* devotion not prepare me for the challenges I faced in the coming years as a new mom, its rose-colored doctrine also supplied me with plenty of damaging illusions."[1]

What if God isn't asking you to lean in? It would be easy to read the principles in this book and think I'm preaching a message to work harder or work smarter. Don't hear what I'm not saying! I challenge you to embrace the range of roles and responsibilities God has for you. I believe the world will become a healthier, more beautiful place as more Christian women leverage their vocational power to love God and serve their neighbors. But that work must be done in God's ways and through his strength. Instead of leaning in, he invites you to *lean hard*.

Ironically, Octavius Winslow, a nineteenth-century male preacher, speaks to the pressures twenty-first-century working women face. In his sermon, "Lean Hard," which includes a beautiful poem by the same name, he captures my desire for you. As I conclude, let Winslow's words serve as a blessing and benediction for your work:

> It is by an act of simple, prayerful faith we transfer our cares and anxieties, our sorrows and wants, to the Lord. . . . [Jesus] invites you come and lean upon Him, and to lean with all your might upon that arm that balances the universe, and upon that bosom that bled for you upon the soldier's spear. . . . Jesus stands at your side and lovingly says—"Cast your burden upon *Me* and

I will sustain thee. I am God Almighty. I bore the load of thy sin and condemnation up the steep of Calvary, and the same power of omnipotence, and the same strength of love that bore it all for thee then, is prepared to bear thy care, and want, and sorrow *now*. Roll it all upon Me."[2]

I invite you to follow Winslow's exhortation and lean hard on the Lord. Whether this season finds you inspired and excited to take on new challenges at work or worn by the pressures you face, Christ stands ready to support you. Instead of following the world's pattern of leaning in to advance yourself through your own effort, lean hard on the Lord and allow his love to guide and sustain you.

Lean Hard

Child of my Love! lean hard,
And let me feel the pressure of thy care.
I know thy burden, child! I shaped it—
Poised it in mine own hand—made no proportion
Of its weight to thine unaided strength;
For even as I laid it on, I said—
"I shall be near, and while she leans on me
This burden shall be mine, not hers;
So shall I keep my child within the circling arms
Of mine own love." Here lay it down: nor fear

To impose it on a shoulder which upholds
The government of worlds. Yet closer come!
Though art not near enough: I would embrace thy care,
So I might feel my child reposing on my breast.
Though lovest me! I know it. Doubt not, then;
But—loving me—*lean hard.*[3]

Spend a few minutes praying through this poem. How is
God asking you to lean on him in this season?

REFLECT

Winslow suggests that God allows us to experience burdens
that only he can carry. What pressures are you carrying alone?

God promises to sustain us when we cast our burdens on him.
What keeps you from fully trusting God with your gifts, leadership, or career?

Identify three key takeaways from this book that you will apply
to your work. Record practical steps you will take to act on
each takeaway and the method and time frame in which you
will do them.

Acknowledgments

This book would not be possible without the Denver Institute for Faith & Work staff team, including its founder, Jeff Haanen. From our first Women, Work & Calling event, you saw the importance of this initiative and celebrated its growth. The way you live with and for God inspires me. Thank you to Lydia Shoaf, who lent her editorial eye to the early stages of this manuscript.

I am grateful for friends like Ingrid Kutsch, who have been tireless champions in my career. Your insight, encouragement, and the occasional push moved me through stuck places and fear. For the "Pheebs" (Denise, Kara, Lisa, Michaela, Missy, and Stephanie) who form a community of friendship and professional excellence that I wish every reader could experience. And for Rick Pratte, Bill Kollar, and JD Punch, good men who affirmed my gifts as a young leader and made space for my leadership alongside their own.

Life would be a lesser place without my family, both biological and adopted. Thank you to the Woods and Sauers, for open homes and listening ears. To Rich and Kirsten Lasinski, for providing the ballast and joy I needed to make it through tumultuous years. And to my mother, Lynda Meyer, a friend, warrior, and encourager. You exemplify faithfulness and love at every stage of your call.

Notes

INTRODUCTION

[1]Some of the book's content appears online in Joanna Meyer's four-part series, "Called Together: A Biblical Perspective on Gender Roles in the Workplace," Denver Institute for Faith & Work (website), May 15, 2018, https://denverinstitute.org/biblical-perspective-gender-roles-1.

1. CALLED TOGETHER

[1]Denise Daniels, "Better Together: Building A Workplace Where Both Men & Women Thrive," (Workshop, Business for the Common Good, Denver, CO, February 1, 2018).

[2]Myk Habets and Beulah Wood, *Reconsidering Gender: Evangelical Perspectives*, (Eugene, OR: Pickwick Publications, 2010), 18.

[3]Daniel J. Sandberg, "When Women Lead, Firms Win," Quantamental Research. October 16, 2019, www.spglobal.com/en/research-insights/featured/special-editorial/when-women-lead-firms-win.

3. CULTURAL NORMS VERSUS BIBLICAL NORMS

[1]Nancy R. Pearcey, *Love Thy Body: Answering Hard Questions about Life and Sexuality.* (Grand Rapids, MI: Baker Books, 2018), 217.

[2]Melissa Russell, "Executive Interview" (interview at Women, Work & Calling conference, Denver, CO, October 23, 2021).

4. WHAT IT MEANS TO BE CALLED

[1]Kate Harris, "The Heart of Vocation," Washington Institute for Faith, Vocation and Culture, accessed February 3, 2023, https://washingtoninst.org/the-heart-of-vocation.

[2]A detailed explanation of predestination exceeds the purposes of this book (and the theological mastery of its author). We believe that an omniscient God knows all the details of our lives before they happen and guides us in any circumstance. However, we are active partners as we cocreate our lives with him.

[3]Os Guinness, *The Call: Finding and Fulfilling the Central Purpose of Your Life* (Nashville, TN: Thomas Nelson, 1998), 42, Kindle.

[4]Tod Bolsinger, "Formed Not Found," Fuller Studio, accessed March 17,2023, https://fullerstudio.fuller.edu/formed-not-found.

5. TOOLS TO EXPLORE YOUR CALLING

[1]Os Guinness, *The Call: Finding and Fulfilling the Central Purpose of Your Life* (Nashville, TN: Thomas Nelson, 1998), 145, Kindle.

[2]Katie Macc, "Living Our Callings: An Iterative Process," (presentation, Women, Work & Calling conference, Denver, CO, October 23, 2021).

6. IDENTIFY BELIEFS THAT LIMIT YOUR GROWTH

[1]Denver Institute for Faith & Work, "How to Overcome the Limiting Beliefs about Your Work with Charlena Ortiz," *Faith & Work Podcast*, July 8, 2021, https://denverinstitute.org/how-to-overcome-the-limiting-beliefs-about-your-work.

7. GOD GROWS YOUR SOUL THROUGH WORK

[1]Mindy Caliguire, "Experiencing Christ Through Our Callings," (presentation, Women, Work & Calling conference, online, October 24, 2020).

8. CULTIVATE HUMBLE CONFIDENCE

[1]Denver Institute for Faith & Work, "How to Have Humble Confidence in the Age of the Personal Brand with Jena Viviano Dunay," *Faith & Work Podcast*, July 15, 2021, https://denverinstitute .org/how-to-have-humble-confidence-in-the-age-of-the-personal -the-personal-brand.

9. OVERCOME IMPOSTOR SYNDROME

[1]Pauline Rose Clance and Suzanne Ament Imes, "The Imposter Phenomenon in High Achieving Women: Dynamics and Therapeutic Intervention," *Psychotherapy: Theory, Research & Practice*, 15 (1978): 241-47, https://doi.org/10.1037/h0086006.

[2]Merritt Onsa, "Women, Use Your Voice," (panel discussion, Women, Work & Calling conference, Denver, CO, October 23, 2021).

[3]Carol Dweck, "What Having a 'Growth Mindset' Means," *Harvard Business Review*, January 13, 2016, https://hbr.org/2016/01 /what-having-a-growth-mindset-actually-means.

10. DISCOVER GOD'S GIFT OF REST

[1]Sarah DiGiulio, "Work Has Fully Invaded Our Personal Lives. Here Are 8 Ways We Can Work Smarter in 2020," BETTER by TODAY, January 2, 2020, www.nbcnews.com/better/lifestyle /work-has-fully-invaded-our-personal-lives-here-are-8 -ncna1108756.

[2]Timothy Keller with Katherine Leary Alsdorf, *Every Good Endeavor: Connecting Your Work to God's Work* (New York: Penguin Books, 2012), 235.

[3]Tara Owens, "Entering Sacred Time: Sabbath, Rest, & Experiencing Time Enough for Everything," (presentation, Women, Work & Calling conference, Denver, CO, October 24, 2018).

11. LEAD WITH AUTHENTICITY AND INTENTIONALITY

[1]Michael Baliousis, Stephen Joseph, P. Alex Linley, John Maltby, and Alex M. Wood, "The Authentic Personality: A Theoretical and Empirical Conceptualization and the Development of the Authenticity Scale," *Journal of Counseling Psychology* 55 (2008), 385-99, https://doi.org/10.1037/0022-0167.55.3.385.

[2]Quoted in Daniel Henderson, *The Prayer God Loves to Answer: Accessing Christ's Wisdom for Your Greatest Need* (Bloomington, MN: Bethany House Publishers, 2016), chap. 9.

[3]Charisse Jones, "Identity, Authenticity, & Mission," (presentation, Women, Work & Calling, conference, Denver, CO, October 23, 2021).

12. REALIZE YOUR VOCATIONAL POWER

[1]Lee Hardy, *The Fabric of This World: Inquiries into Calling, Career Choice, and The Design of Human Work* (Grand Rapids, MI: Eerdmans, 1990), 83.

[2]Amy Sherman, *Kingdom Calling: Vocational Stewardship for the Common Good* (Downers Grove, IL: InterVarsity Press, 2011), chap. 9.

13. RESIST THE NEED TO BE PERFECT

[1]Mary Ward, "Women More Likely to Be Perfectionists, Anxious at Work," *Sydney Morning Herald*, April 17, 2018.

[2]Jessica Bennett, "It's Not You, It's Science: How Perfectionism Holds Women Back," *Time*, April 22, 2014, https://time.com/70558/its-not-you-its-science-how-perfectionism-holds-women-back.

[3]Jo Saxton, "Becoming a Relationally Generous Leader," (presentation, Women, Work & Calling conference, Denver, CO, October 23, 2021).

[4]Saxton, "Relationally Generous Leader."

15. BE AWARE OF THE DOUBLE BIND

[1]Nicholas Kristof, "When Women Rule," *New York Times*, February 10, 2008, www.nytimes.com/2008/02/10/opinion/10kristof.html.

[2]Deborah Streeter, "Women in Leadership: Navigating the Double Bind" (course, Women in Leadership Certificate, Cornell University, March 13, 2022).

16. RE-ENVISION MENTORSHIP

[1]Stephanie Summers, "Better Together: Discovering the Power of Networks," (panel discussion, Women, Work & Calling conference, Denver, CO, October 23, 2021).

[2]Laura Flanders, "Busting Myths about Mentoring," *Faith & Work Podcast*, February 25, 2022, https://denverinstitute.org/busting-myths-about-mentoring.

[3]Flanders, "Busting Myths."

[4]Denise Daniels, "Better Together: Building A Workplace Where Both Men & Women Thrive," (workshop, Business for the Common Good conference, Denver, CO, February 1, 2018).

17. NETWORK IN NEW WAYS

[1]Greg Lewis, "LinkedIn Data Shows Women Are Less Likely to Have Strong Relationships–Here's What Companies Should Do," *LinkedIn Talent Blog*, March 11, 2020, www.linkedin.com/business/talent/blog/talent-acquisition/women-less-likely-to-have-strong-networks.

[2]Lou Adler, "New Survey Reveals 85% of Jobs Are Filled by Networking," LinkedIn, February 28, 2016, www.linkedin.com/pulse/new-survey-reveals-85-all-jobs-filled-via-networking-lou-adler.

[3]Makisha Boothe, "Better Together: Discovering the Power of Networks," (panel discussion with Sarah Lampard and Stephanie Summers at Women, Work & Calling conference, Denver, CO, October 23, 2021).

[4]Sarah Lampard, "Better Together: Discovering the Power of Networks," (panel discussion with Makisha Boothe and Stephanie Summers at Women, Work & Calling conference, Denver, CO, October 23, 2021).

[5]Boothe, "Better Together."

[6]Stephanie Summers, "Better Together: Discovering the Power of Networks," (panel discussion with Makisha Boothe and Sarah Lampard at Women, Work & Calling conference, Denver, CO, October 23, 2021).

[7]Amy Poehler, *Yes Please* (New York: Harper Collins, 2014), 149.

18. BECOME A RELATIONALLY GENEROUS WOMAN

[1]Jo Saxton, "Becoming a Relationally Generous Leader," (presentation at Women, Work & Calling conference, Denver, CO, October 23, 2021).

²Julia Eilperin, "White House Women Want to Be in the Room Where It Happens," *Washington Post*, September 13, 2016, www .washingtonpost.com/news/powerpost/wp/2016/09/13/white -house-women-are-now-in-the-room-where-it-happens.

³Saxton, "Relationally Generous Leader."

19. RESTORE THE BLESSED ALLIANCE

¹Carolyn Custis James, "The Blessed Alliance," Carolyn Custis James (website), September 18, 2012, https://carolyncustisjames .com/2012/09/18/the-blessed-alliance.

²Custis James, "Blessed Alliance."

20. DON'T LEAN IN, LEAN HARD

¹Katherine Goldstein, "I Was a Sheryl Sandberg Superfan. Then Her 'Lean In' Advice Failed Me," *Vox*, December 6, 2018, www .vox.com/first-person/2018/12/6/18128838/michelle-obama -lean-in-sheryl-sandberg.

²Octavius Winslow, *The Ministry of Home; Or, Brief Expository Lectures on Divine Truth* (London: William Hunt and Company, 1867), 354-55, www.google.com/books/edition/The_Ministry _of_Home_Or_Brief_Expository/uOhoAAAAcAAJ?hl=en &gbpv=1.

³Winslow, *The Ministry of Home*, 355.

ABOUT DENVER INSTITUTE FOR FAITH & WORK

Over a lifetime, most of us will spend more than ninety thousand hours at work, but we often miss what God has to say about work's purpose and mission. We believe individuals, families, and communities thrive when people envision their daily work as an opportunity to join God in his work to make all things new. At Denver Institute for Faith & Work we work to see people formed to serve God, neighbor, and society through their daily work. In our public engagement initiatives, thought leadership, the *Faith & Work Podcast*, and programs like the 5280 and CityGate Fellowships, we help people live with God, for the world, through their daily work.

Women, Work & Calling is a nationally focused initiative led by Denver Institute that equips Christian women for godly influence in public life through our annual event of the same name, publications, and relationally rich learning experiences.

Learn more at **www.denverinstitute.org**,
find us on social media **@DenverInstitute**,
and check out **www.womenworkandcalling.com**.